Want a Commute of 30 Seconds?

Tracey Leak

This book is copyright. Apart from any fair dealing for the purposes of private study, research or review, as permitted under the Copyright Act, no part may be reproduced by any process or distributed without written permission from the publisher or author.

The information provided in this book 'Want a commute of 30 seconds?' is intended as suggestions only. Our services are advisory only. Any view or opinions expressed from or during interviews are those of the individuals speaking and do not necessarily represent the views or opinions of the author (Tracey Leak of Tracelle Enterprises Pty Ltd) or any of its affiliates or employees. This information is not intended to be a substitute for gaining specific professional advice from legal, tax, investment, accounting, insurance, or financial advisors. It is the reader's responsibility to consult professional advice or services with regard to any strategies outlined in this book and to determine their relevance to the reader's geographical location and personal situation. The contents of this book in no way dilute the absolute responsibility of the reader to perform due diligence with regard to any transactions nor do they absolve the reader from, or assign to the author, responsibility for the consequences of any actions taken.

Cover design: Alvin T. Cruz
Cover Photo: Steven Caldwell Entertainment
Tracey's photo (back cover): Nick McAlinden, Imago Photography
Editor: Kim McKenzie ☺

www.TheArtOfHomeBasedBusiness.com

Copyright © 2012 Tracey Leak and Tracelle Enterprises P/L
All Rights Reserved.

With Thanks . . . .

> For my Mum, who has no idea how much she has positively impacted my life by leading the way in her own home-based business. I love and admire her more than words can express.

Look for ways to add value . . .

Tracey Leak grew up in country Australia in a home-based business. She started her first business when she was just seven years old.

Tracey lived in Canada for a year on a Rotary Youth Exchange, returning to Australia to complete high school before completing a Bachelor of Applied Science at the Royal Melbourne Institute of Technology.

Working as a radiographer, Tracey was unable to ignore the entrepreneur in her heart. After being diagnosed with a brain tumour, which she no longer has, she made her leap into being a full-time small business owner.

Tracey's journey led her to become a business coach after much coaxing from her own business coach. Seven and a half years after helping many business owners find their success, Tracey has returned to her childhood roots as a specialist in home-based business.

Tracey still works from home on the Gold Coast, Australia and can be found most days in her PJ's.

Check out Tracey's <u>FREE</u> webinar, download your <u>FREE</u> e-book (Which Home-Based Business?) and The Art of Home-Based Business <u>FREE</u> e-magazine!

www.TheArtOfHomeBasedBusiness.com

Contents:

1	Want a commute of 30 seconds?
5	Why this book?
8	There are only four areas you need to work on
9	The first area
12	The second area
14	The third area
16	The fourth area
19	Part 1: Why?
33	Part 2: Skill
38	Let's start with marketing
49	Sales
53	One last word on skills
55	Part 3: Mindset
71	Part 4: Action
78	Time management
85	Work Ethic
89	Final Words

WANT A COMMUTE OF 30 SECONDS?

Want a Commute of 30 Seconds?

A question I get asked a lot is how long does it take me to get to work in the morning? My response is simple - it all depends on where I am in my home! If I'm in the kitchen, it is about 10 seconds, from the bedroom, maybe 15 seconds.

It's the dream, right? Working from home, no boss to answer to, no wasting time stuck in peak hour traffic. What would your life be like if you could work from home? This is a joy I've experienced for coming up to eight years.

As technology improves, we are more connected than ever, so why is it that more and more people feel disconnected from their own lives? No longer can a family live easily on a single income as living expenses increase. The demand on our time is also higher than ever. More and more children are left to be cared for in day care centres whilst their parents are out working to provide an income for their family.

Although we are busier than ever, we are losing the feeling that we are in control of our lives and freedom is a dream that often feels like it will never be fulfilled. What is the answer? Your own home-based business.

Home-based businesses come in so many different forms and there are so many opportunities, I always wonder why everyone doesn't have one. You may choose to build a home business full-time, or maybe one part-time to add to your income whilst starting to work towards you goals, hopes and dreams for your life.

What can you do from home? The choices are endless from service providing businesses like a virtual assistant, bookkeeper or consultant, to e-commerce stores, party plan, manufacturing, network marketing and information marketing. But it is not what to do that stops many people from getting started in their own home-based business. It is more likely their belief in themselves.

That is why I've written this book. It's not all about your mindset, in fact that is just one part. It is about the basics of a home-based business to help you.

For those of you who dream of a home-based business, this book will not only give you the foundations to build from, but the belief and maybe even the motivation to get started.

For those already in a home-based business, then I hope this book adds value to you, and that you take these basics and build to the next level in your business.

Why this book . . . . .

My story is a little different from most and it is the reason why I am so passionate about helping people, in particular parents, in home-based business.

I grew up in a home-based business. My Mum owned a manufacturing business making school uniforms. She started with just one school and built that business up to make uniforms for nearly every school in the state. She owned and operated that business for nearly 34 years – she started it when I was just six months old.

Dad also owned and operated his own businesses and eventually joined Mum in her business as it grew to a point where it took both of them to operate it. In fact, for many years, it was my Mum who was the major bread winner in our household.

If you ask my Mum, she will probably tell you that she was working all the time as we grew up and that her business took a lot of her time to run and grow. What I remember is a different story. I remember Mum always being there. We would come home from school and head out to her workshop in our backyard (lovingly called "The Dungeon") and chat to her whilst she worked. Many of my school holidays were spent working for her – at slave labour rates of course!

Now, years later as I work with clients in my business coaching, I have discovered what a difference it made to me and how I think, because I grew up "in business". There is a noticeable difference in people whose parents were employees (which I often refer to as the 'first generation entrepreneurs') to those who had parents that were business owners.

For people who are the first generation in their family to get into business, it can sometimes be a big jump to break the bonds of employee thinking. If you grew up with parents that were employees, then you are forging a new path in your own business. You have no example to work by, no innate compass to direct you. I, on the other hand, grew up with parents in a business and not just any business, but a home-based business. I saw and heard everything first hand. As a child of entrepreneurial parents I learnt by watching and by being in the centre of an environment that showed me what I needed to do to run a business. I think differently to a first generation entrepreneur.

This does not make me better or more successful than a first generation entrepreneur, but it does make me more willing to have a go, take risks and realise that if I want to be successful, I need to make it happen.

So why this book? Because it's about where my passion lies, it's to do with children. I love helping children to learn and grow. Sometimes we even joke that I communicate better with kids than adults! What is the best way I can help children? By using my skills and talents to help parents in business, their children will get to experience what I did – having their parents at home with them. Secondly, they will be growing up with a slightly different mindset because they will be learning to have personal responsibility for all aspects of their lives. In business it is totally up to you to make it happen.

I believe that I will never see the result of my work. By helping parents during my life, they will be able to bring up their children just a little bit differently. This in turn means they will bring up their children just a little bit differently, who will do the same for the next generation and the generation after that. It's the butterfly effect.

So now you know why I've written this book, but now it's time to put the focus back on you.

How much do you want to get back your freedom? How much do you want to reduce the stress in your life and gain control back on your time and finances?

Within the pages of this book, even though it is not that big, are the ideas and lessons you need to gain success in a home-based business.

Are you ready to join me on the 30 second commute?

There are only 4 areas you need to work on . . . . .

In today's world where things are seeming to become more advanced and more complicated, I want to simplify home-based business for you so that you can see that it is not only a great way to work and live your life, but that it can also be easy.

As a business coach, I work a lot with large franchise groups. People spend thousands, if not hundreds of thousands, to buy a business within a franchise group. What are they actually buying? A system on how to run their new business. What's the number one thing I see these franchise business owners do? Not follow the system!

This can be said for even lower entry cost businesses like network marketing or party plan businesses. There is a proven system that works, yet when people enter into these businesses they spend all their time trying to 'improve' the system or finding faults with the system and focusing on why it won't work for them, rather than just following the system. In fact, the only thing that's not working is them!

Whether you are in a franchise business or a business with a system like a party plan or network marketing business (which by the way, have the exact same structure and principles as the hundreds of thousands of dollars franchise businesses) or you are starting your own home-based business from scratch, there is a general business system to follow. I want to share that with you in this book and it comes down to four key areas that you need to work on.

The first area . . .

The first area you need to work on is SKILL – the skills of business. This includes marketing, sales, operations, finance, management, and any of the areas you may need to work on your business.

As a business coach, when people approach me about helping them in their business, this is usually the first area people think they need to work on. They will say things like, "I'm not very good at selling. Can you teach me how to sell?" or "I don't know how to market my business. I don't have a marketing degree. Can you teach me how to be a better marketer?"

In the end, skill is not the most important thing in a home-based business, or any business for that matter. Yes, there are certain skills you require, but it isn't the most important area.

I like to remind people (and I'll remind you right now as well) is to remember that a <u>skill is something that can be learned</u>. That is the definition of skill. It is not something you are born with or unique only to you, it is something that can be learned. So yes, in your business you will need to learn the skills of business, but the big thing to realise is that you can learn them.

Which skills should you learn first? I am going to take you through the skills that will have the biggest impact on your business in our skills chapter in this book, but I have an idea for you first.

If you had a teenager in school and they were excelling at art, with straight A's, but they were borderline passing in math, which subject would the majority of the population recommend we get a tutor for to help this student?

Most people would say maths. Why? Because obviously they need help with it as it is their weakness. I, on the other hand have a different thought of this. This student is never going to be a mathematician. They obviously don't have a talent for maths. Sure, if they need a tutor to get the basics and to pass the subject then get them one, but it isn't going to have a massive impact on their life. On the other hand though, what if we got them a tutor for art? They are displaying a natural talent so why not foster this talent and develop it? Not only will it build their skill, I think it will be far more enjoyable for the student *plus* it will generate a bigger result.

Now think of you in your business. What skills are you trying to improve? Are you working on the areas that you are already displaying a natural talent in or the areas you love to work on, or are you focusing just on your weaknesses?

Work on your strengths if you want to gain greater success.

Here's an example. I know many business owners that just love people. It is their favourite part of their business to meet with their clients, or to go out to networking events and to meet new people. They love connecting with them. This is their strength and more than likely their natural talent. From what I have observed personally these same business owners, generally hate doing their books, their accounting and the detailed paperwork of their business. So should they take a bookkeeping course and improve their skills as a bookkeeper, or would it just be better for them to outsource this task to someone who does actually have the talent in this area, allowing them to focus on getting out and meeting more people? I hope you agree with me that the latter is the better option for them.

Take a minute right now and work out what your talents are in your home-based business? What are the tasks or areas you love to do? Now, think about what you could do to improve these areas by just 10%? How different would your business be? How much more fun would you be having in your business?

Unfortunately it is also true, that in a home-based business you are still going to have to do a few things that are not your strengths or high on your enjoyment list, but I'll help you with those a bit later on.

The second area . . .

Although skill is important, and an area you need to work on in your business, it isn't the only area or the most vital. The next area you need to work on is MINDSET.

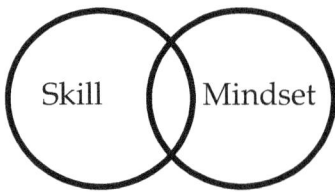

Mindset is not just about having a positive attitude. It is also about how you react and respond to situations or challenges as they arise (and they will) in your home-based business.

For home-based business owners, I believe this is of even more importance than it is for other types of businesses to focus on. Why? Because home-based business is often a solitary endeavour. There will be a lot of times when you will be working alone and it will be only your voice that you will be hearing inside your head. Sometimes it can feel like there is more than one voice in there too!

You are 100% responsible for your mindset. It is up to you to keep going when you want to quit. It is up to you to pick yourself up after you have fallen down. Remember though, it is also up to you to allow yourself to succeed. It is up to you to not sabotage yourself when things are going well. It is up to you to believe that you are worthy of having all of your life's dreams and goals.

This is something I've discovered over the last eight years working as a home-based business owner and whilst working with my clients. When an individual enters into a business, by nature they are more than willing to be 100% responsible when things don't go right in their business or life, but very few will take this same viewpoint when things go well or there is success. They will play down their success or hand over the ownership of their success to things such as "luck" or a "bit of a fluke" or that it wasn't really anything "special" that they did. Although you don't want to have an over-inflated ego way of thinking and telling everyone how great you are, there is a big chasm of space between an over-inflated ego and accepting that you have done something great.

Although mindset is vitally important and something you need to consider and work on in your home-based business, I still don't think it is the most important area of your business.

The third area . . . .

It is great to have excellent skills in business and it is awesome to have a positive mindset, but it won't produce success in your home-based business, because if you don't do anything, nothing will happen. For this you need ACTION.

You need to take action to gain success in your business. I am totally for the law of attraction and believe and use this in my daily life, but the thing to remember is that you can't sit on your couch saying affirmations and hoping that they will come true. You need to get out and take action, to start doing the work to follow up on your affirmations.

Because a home-based business is often reliant on you, it is vitally important that you do the work that is required. Work ethic is a vital and key part of your business and you need to get out onto the path towards success.

The biggest problem is that in society, work is almost a dirty word. When you think of the word "work", what comes to mind? We often think of "work" as being hard, boring, something you have to do and that it's not enjoyable. Why would anyone want to do something that they think is not going to be fun or something that is simply a "have to do" item? I want you to start flipping this around. Work is just work. It is up to you to either make it fun or boring. It is up to you if you see work as something exciting to do or something that is a necessary evil.

I love my "work". I can't wait to get started each and every day. This is not because I am some sort of weird freak, it is because I have decided to make it that way. You will understand this more in a minute.

So let's all just agree right now that if you want to build a business it is going to take some work. Do you know the old saying, "The only place where success comes before work is in the dictionary"? It is so true.

So action is important to your home-based business, but guess what? I don't think it is the most important thing in your business.

The fourth area....

As you can see from my diagram, the three areas we have looked at – skill, mindset and action – overlap. In fact, the more skills you have, the more action you take and the better your mindset is, the more they will overlap and will result in you having greater success in your home-based business.

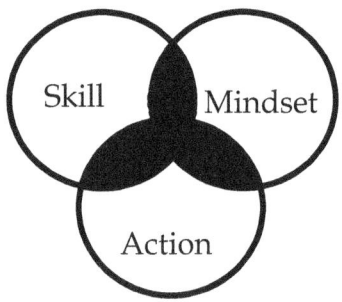

I like to think of these three areas in this diagram as balloons. Just as with real balloons, there is nothing that holds them together and each area could simply 'float away'.

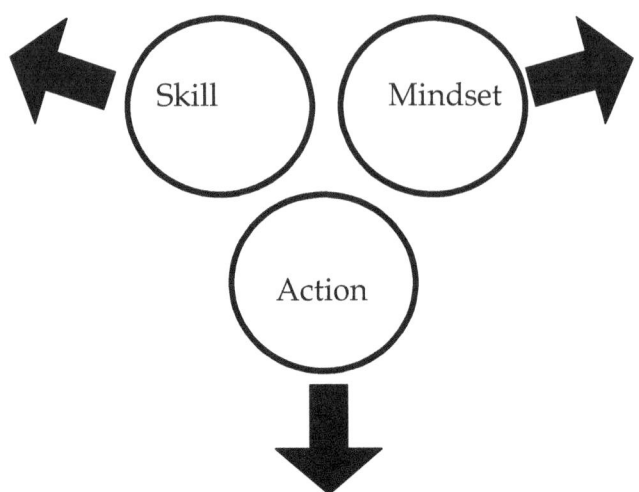

Imagine that one day you get up and your mindset is negative. You mindset 'balloon' has drifted away or maybe you take on a new client and you just don't have the skills to service them so your skill 'balloon' floats away or maybe you just don't take any action so therefore your action 'balloon' is separated from your skills and mindset 'balloons'. Without some sort of frame to hold these three areas together, you will not gain the success you are looking for in your business.

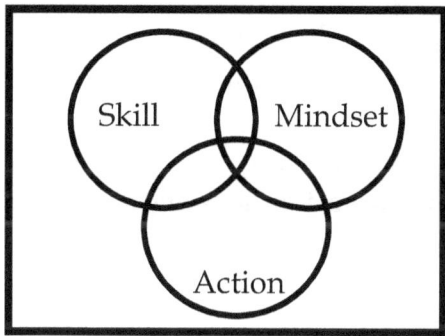

So what is this frame that will hold these areas together? It is your WHY? Why are you doing this business? What is it you want it to provide or produce for your life? Who is it you want to serve? Why?

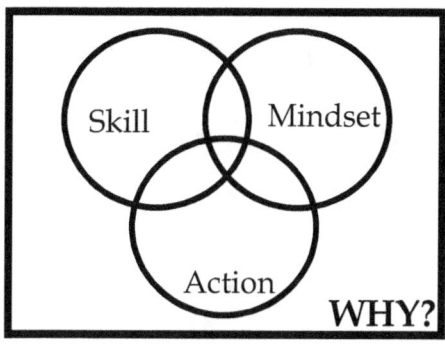

I believe this to be the most important word in your business – <u>WHY</u>? It is also the least asked question and it shouldn't be!

Your business should be the vehicle to produce the life you want to live, it isn't supposed to be your life. The problem is that most people don't stop and really ask themselves what they want in their life, or give it the thought it deserves.

Without a strong 'why', you will never do the work required to build your business. Without a strong 'why', you will never develop the skills you need to run your business. Without a strong 'why', when things go wrong (and they will) and your mindset turns negative, you will not pick yourself up and work through your challenges. A strong 'why' will help you get through the darkest of days and will allow you to enjoy the days when everything is going your way.

Your 'why' is the most important thing in your business. So let's talk about your 'why'…..

Part 1:

WHY?

WHY?

It sounds good in theory that you need to have a strong 'why', but for some people it can be very, very hard to discover what that 'why' is.

I get told by so many people that they are in business because they want to be a millionaire. That's their 'why'. You might be reading this and thinking, "Tracey, isn't that a good enough reason to be in business?" Of course it is good enough, but is it the best reason?

Your 'why' shouldn't be a 'thing', it should be more of a feeling. A million dollars is a thing, not a feeling. Unless you are like Scrooge McDuck who wants to sit in a vault of money, a 'why' of a million dollars is not enough.

When things get tough – which they will – you will talk yourself around and say things like, 'Well, I don't really need a million dollars. I just need enough money to survive' or maybe even 'Who wants to be a millionaire anyway?' Money is not a 'why'.

In the end, money is just the currency we use to exchange for goods and services. If we lived hundreds of years ago they used to use other things instead of money as a currency from beads to pigs. Money is not a 'why'.

Take the idea that the reason you are in your business is to make a million dollars. All I would like to ask you is why? Why a million dollars? What does a million dollars mean to you? If you can, go ahead right now and write down what you would do if your business made a million dollars profit. What would you use that money for?

I'm going to use a common response as an example for you. I often get the response that "I would pay out the mortgage on our house so that we could live mortgage free". That is getting much closer to a 'why' for sure and a great way to use your million dollars, but I still want to know why? Why would you choose to pay your house off?

What are the words that have come to mind just as you have read that? Did words like security, freedom, peace of mind or something similar float through your head?

Your 'why' is not to make a million dollars. Your 'why' is not to pay off your house. These are action steps or goals to be achieved. Your 'why' could be something like "To have the peace of mind that my family is financially secure which gives me a sense of freedom".

Does that *feel* a little different to "I want to make a million dollars"? Your 'why' is not something you think in your head, it is something you feel in your body. My 'why' is like a burning in my gut. It almost has a life of its own because I want it so much. If you don't feel that burning desire to achieve and have your 'why', then quite bluntly, you are just not going to do what it takes to achieve it.

I know that this is harsh, but it is also true. If your 'why' isn't strong inside of you, when things get tough and you are not sure if you can get up one more time, or even make one more phone call, or do something a little out of your comfort zone, you will quit. You won't achieve what it is you want for your life.

So how do you discover this 'why'? Whilst I was researching the different methods of discovering your 'why' or how to find your life purpose and achieving goals, I came across an exercise on the internet. I never wrote down where I found this so I apologise right now to the person who should be given credit for this exercise, but it is the one exercise that I've found anyone can do. In all the years I've used it, it has never failed me or anyone I've done it with.

Get out a sheet of blank paper, preferably not lined and grab a pen. Make sure you find a pen that is in good working order so that you are not distracted by a pen running out of ink! I learnt that lesson the hard way!

Next you have to find a quiet place where you will not be interrupted for at least thirty minutes. It only took me three minutes to do this exercise, but if you haven't done anything like this before, then you may need some extra time.

Now put pen to paper. At the top of the page I want you to write 'What do I really want?' Then, start writing. Start writing everything you want, but remember to always ask the question why? If you write down I want to pay off my house, then ask yourself why and write that down. Keep writing. Get it all out. What do you really want – in life! This is not just about business, but about all aspects of your life. What is your purpose in life? What do you want to achieve? Who do you want to help? What do you want for your kids? Constantly keep asking yourself why?

How do you know when you have got your answer? It will bring tears to your eyes, you will feel a burning or sometimes churning in your gut, it will make you *feel*. I don't care if you are the toughest, meanest bloke in the world, it should bring tears to your eyes. When you want it so much and you can feel it burning through you (in a good way), that is your 'why'.

Please stop now and do this exercise. Without it, you won't get the full advantage of this book and you definitely won't be taking full advantage of your life. Life is far too short to waste another minute not understanding what your 'why' is.

I had a life event that changed my life. I was diagnosed with a brain tumour. It was a massive wake up call for me to start living my life and to not just *exist* through my life. I don't want you to have to have a life event to make you connect to your reason for your life.

This may seem a little deep when you are thinking, "But I just want to make a couple of extra hundred dollars a week so that I don't have to put my kids in childcare and go to a job". But trust me when I say, if you don't know your 'why', you may make your couple of extra hundred dollars a week, but you won't do more than that, you won't be truly living your life and it won't be as rewarding.

So do you know what your 'why' is yet?

Next, you want to ask yourself the question, "Is this home-based business going to help me to fulfill my 'why'? Is it a great starting point for me?" If you are not yet in a home-based business then I have a free e-book to help you discover which home-based business is right for you. Go to my website (www.theartofhomebasedbusiness.com) and download it free of charge.

I think it is important to stop and ask if your current or proposed business will get you to your 'why', because I sit with a lot of business owners that want something for their life, but their current business is just never going to provide it. Think of your business like it's a sports car. It is very cool, it goes fast and is a great car to drive. The problem is, if you want to go to the island just off the coast, that car, no matter how cool it is, no matter how fast it goes, is not going to get very far before it sinks to the bottom of the ocean. The best way to get to that island might be a rusty old barge. Too often business owners want something for their lives or have a 'why' that their business is just never going to provide. Now is the time to ask that question yourself.

A lot of people have the perception that when you are in a home-based business that all you do is work from your home and never venture out the door. Just because a business is home-based, doesn't mean it has to be home-bound. If you discovered your 'why' had something to do with people, then it doesn't mean you need to go set up a commercial office, you can still work from home. Your home is your base of operations.

At one stage in my business coaching, we had an office. It was a very nice office on a very prestigious street in Brisbane, but did we need it? No. In fact, if any of my clients did come to see me, we didn't sit in the office, we went to a coffee shop on the street. When we decided to move our operations back to a home-base, I had a client call me and say that he was going to be near the 'office' for another appointment before our normal phone coaching session so would I like to meet him at the coffee shop instead? That was ten months after we had moved out of the office. He had completely forgotten that I worked from home.

Your 'why' is far more important than where you base your business. If your 'why' includes your partner, your children, your family, then doesn't it make perfect sense to be home-based?

I want to cover one point before I go on any further. This is particularly so for women. Many women (and when I say many, I mean lots and lots of women) ask me the question of "Can I be a good mother AND run my own business? If I have my own business, won't that mean that I'm not being the best mother I can be?"

I'm not going to give you research or theory as an answer, I am going to give you actual proof that not only can you do it, it will actually make you a better mother.

How do I have that proof? Because I am the proof. I don't remember my Mum 'working', I remember my Mum being there whenever I needed her (and even when I didn't). I saw my Mum doing what she loved. I saw my Mum going after her own goals. I saw my Mum display work ethic. Remember, your kids don't learn from what you tell them, they learn from watching what you do. I think it would be much harder, not impossible, but harder to be a 'good' Mum by going to a job every day. Become an 'and' woman and you can do both!

Now you have your 'why', what do you do with it? It is time to work on your goals and dreams. Did you know that the figures say only 3% of the population have written goals? I am amazed every time I read or hear that fact, because I just don't know how people get any sort of traction in their lives to achieve things without having them written down.

There are so many books on goal setting and how to do SMART goals. In case you haven't read one of them, SMART goals are goals that you set out in a specific framework. The goal needs to be Specific, Measurable, Achievable, Realistic or Results orientated and be to a Time frame. These types of goals certainly do work, but I like to make my goals around my 'why'.

Rather than a goal being something you have to achieve, for example, I need to gain 10 new customers by May 3, I like to make it around the 'why'. Sure this goal fits the SMART principle, but it doesn't excite me. It doesn't make me jump up and want to achieve it. Why do I want to gain 10 new customers? What does that really mean to me? What if 10 new customers meant an extra $5,000 of profit a month and that profit meant you could pay an extra $5,000 on your mortgage. That then meant that you would pay your mortgage off in just 5 years instead of 20 years. What would that mean to you? Maybe that then means you are financially secure. So is the goal 10 new customers by May 3 or is the goal to be financially secure? (It's the second one if you didn't work that out!)

When you look at a goal, you need to have action steps to achieve the goal. The 10 new customers is one of the action steps. The goal is your 'why'.

This could be totally different to anything you may have learnt previously about goal setting, but if you don't connect your actions to your 'why', you won't achieve them. If you set a goal that has no meaning to you, you might achieve it, but probably not.

Goal setting is not a hideous task that has to be endured in a business. It should be an exciting process to work out the steps to achieve your 'why'. You should set your goals with a feeling of excitement, a feeling that you are one step closer to your burning desire, your 'why'. If this is not the feeling you are getting, then I'd question if you are setting goals that you think you *should* be doing instead of setting goals and action steps that you *want* to be doing.

The more you want it, the more likely you are going to do what it takes to achieve it. If you are setting goals that you think you *should* be doing or goals to please other people, you may achieve them, but they won't be as rewarding.

As a little side note, if you write a goal and it scares the pants off you, that's OK. I write goals all the time that produce a whole stack of fear, but at the same time, it excites me. Even writing this book was a goal that produced enormous amounts of fear inside me. My English teacher in high school told me I was not very good at the subject, which left me with the belief that I could never write a book. So why am I writing a book? Because my 'why' involves helping home-based business owners. My 'why' is about helping parents be there for their kids. My 'why' is so big inside of me that I will get out of my own way to make it happen. I want and need to help and serve home-based business owners and one of the ways I can do this is to have a book so they can gain access to my knowledge. Why would I let one teacher from over 20 years ago stop me achieving my 'why'? Plus it helps that I have an amazing editor that corrects all my spelling and punctuation errors!

What is stopping you? You need to get honest with yourself and take the time to write down everything that is stopping you from doing what it takes and achieving your why. This is not to depress you, but I find that if we don't know what is stopping you, then we can't overcome it.

Once you have written the list of things that are stopping you, take a minute, preferably with a big fat marker, and cross out every item on that list that is just nonsense. Yes, it is nonsense.

Look at my previous example. Why would one comment from a teacher 20 years ago stop me from achieving my 'why', the thing that is my burning desire? Especially when you realise that I can just find someone with more skill and talent in that area to help me.

What if you think you are not smart enough or don't have the right education? Did you know that Richard Branson has always worked from home? I didn't know that until I saw an interview with him on 'Oprah' and they were talking to his kids and they mentioned that he always worked from home. Go and read Richard Branson's book 'Losing my Virginity' and see what his education was like. I think you will be amazed and inspired.

What if you think, but I'm an introvert and can't be the star of the show. Warren Buffett, currently the third wealthiest man in the world, is an introvert. That didn't stop him.

I interviewed eight home-based business owners from different backgrounds and different businesses about how they turned their home-based businesses into millions of dollars (*Make a Million in your PJ's*). What amazed me was how different they all were, but in the end, they were all very similar. They had a reason to do what they did and then overcame challenges and focused on the end goal. They worked through their weaknesses and focused on their strengths. In the end, it is probably only you that is stopping you from achieving your 'why'.

You have to start to believe that you are worthy of achieving your 'why'. You deserve all the good, happiness and success as much as the next person. It is up to you to believe you are worthy of achieving your goals, dreams and success. This does not mean you are arrogant or self-centered. It is just something you have to allow. Yes, you need to allow yourself to believe you are worthy.

If you are reading these words right now you will be in one of two places. The first one is, "Yes, I'm worthy so get on with it Tracey". The second is, "I'm so not worthy and I kind of feel like crying".

To feel worthy of success is a process. It is not as easy as flicking a switch and it is often something you learnt as a child, not as an adult. So take the time to work on believing you are worthy of success. Start to write down reasons why you are worthy. To get you started, remember that I believe you are worthy.

I have discovered over the many years working with business owners that often times their 'why' is not a selfish thing. Often times it includes their family or their community or the world for that matter. Maybe it is because they are passionate about saving the environment or helping children in a third world country or maybe having freedom in their own life. To say I want to make a million dollars is not a 'why', but if that million dollars means they can provide financial security for their children, then don't you think that it is a good thing? If you don't think you are worthy, that is selfish. If by you thinking you are not worthy, when you are clearly seeking a 'why' that is bigger than you, then why are you stopping it? Believe you are worthy. Start with the decision to just go with it and build it from there.

Before we move onto the skills of business, I want to remind you that to really get traction in your business and achieve your desired success faster and easier, then make sure you are connecting to your 'why' daily. If you can, multiple times throughout the day. That's why vision boards and dream books work so well. By seeing pictures it will invigorate your senses and it can literally put you in the picture. The more you can encompass all of your senses, the more focused you become. Put notes around your house. Write your 'why' down and read and feel it daily. Your 'why' is the framework that will hold your home-based business together and keep it moving forward.

Part 2:
SKILL

SKILL

I love working with people on what I call the 'nuts and bolts' or the basic skills of business. When I started to learn these skills when I first began my own business, it was like I was learning an amazing new language, but the best thing was the skills and ideas behind them were simple.

Kate, who was my coach when I first started in business and now my friend, always used to say to me, "Business is not hard, it is us that makes it hard". The principles of business are simple systems if we let them be and most of the time they are common sense. Learning the skills of business is easy, the question is, will you use them? Then the next question is, will you learn them at the next level and use them again?

When learning the basics of business you do so like it's an onion. The first time you learn them, it is like you are the outer layer of an onion. As you progress in your business you will strip away layers of the onion and learn these same principles on a new level. The biggest mistake business owners make is they confuse time in their business with the skill of business. Just because a business owner has owned and run a business for thirty years, doesn't mean they have thirty years of business experience. More times than not, they have actually run their business for one year and then repeated that year another twenty-nine times, never learning or growing to the next level. That is why some people who have been in business for just three years could have more experience and knowledge than someone that has lasted thirty years.

This means that even though the lessons are the same, each time you learn the nuts and bolts of business it will have a new meaning or a new lesson for you, with new ways to apply those lessons in your business and life. It still excites me to teach the nuts and bolts of business and why that every time I teach them, I too am learning at the next level.

Successful business owners – home-based or not – realise that to continue to have consistent success in their business, they need to continue to grow and learn. If you become stale or stagnant in your growth or learning, your business will quickly shrink and maybe even die.

If you were to build a house, what do you start with? The foundations. You will pour the slab and make sure everything is strong and stable before you even contemplate building up. The same principles apply with business. You have to start from a solid foundation and build from there. When you foundations are strong you can build as big a business as you like. Most business owners don't take the time to build a solid foundation and that's why the majority of businesses fail in their first two years of operation. The first big storm that comes, it knocks their business over.

As I've mentioned before, the first thing to remember is to identify your strengths and talents in your business. This does not mean you can ignore the areas you don't enjoy or you feel are a weakness for you. If you think that you are weak or have poor skills in sales and you don't particularly like it, then you business will not succeed, because without sales you will not have any business or make any profit! Remember, the purpose of a business is to make money. The more you can look at your strengths and make them applicable to *all* areas of your business, the more success you will have.

PART 2: SKILL

In this chapter, I want to cover two of the main areas of business skill that people either love or hate. They are marketing and sales. Both are essential to making your home-based business work, but they are also the two most likely areas where people don't have the skills necessary to grow a strong base to their business.

Of course there are other skill areas that you need to work on such as managing, delivery and distribution, operations, team, finances, vision and planning to name a few, but we will cover the two biggest here.

Let's start with marketing.

When I first started in business, I had no experience in marketing and thought that I needed a degree in marketing to know what to do. I am going to teach you the one thing that I still use whenever I do marketing that will have the greatest effect on generating leads to your business, which is what marketing is for, lead generation.

To do marketing well, the first thing you have to do is to know and understand and be able to relate to your customer. Marketing is all about attracting people to your business. To attract people, you have to know what they like and what they want.

Think about marketing from a bigger perspective. If you are trying to attract a twenty year old female you will be using different words, images and you will find them 'hanging out' in a different location to a sixty year old male? So wouldn't it make sense that the first thing you need to do in marketing is to identify who it is you are trying to attract to your business?

If your home-based business is bookkeeping, then you would want to attract business owners not employees. If your home-based business is selling skin care via party plan, then you would want to attract people who like to use skin care and like to buy in a social environment?

It really is common sense, but the number of business owners I sit with who don't know who they are trying to attract to their business amazes me. The more you know about your customer, the easier it is to attract them.

PART 2: SKILL   39

So step one in marketing is to identify and write out (yes, pen to paper!) WHO is your ideal client.

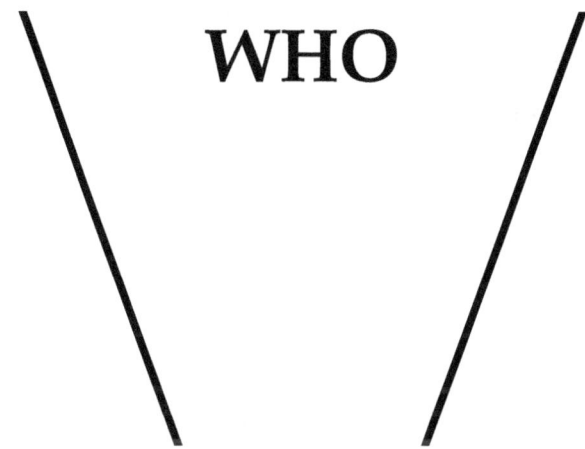

Why do I say ideal rather than target market? I believe that in business you want to really aim for that ideal client, the person who is your perfect customer, the people you really want to help and serve. Sure, if someone comes along that is not perfect or ideal but wants to buy from you, then don't stop them, but don't waste your time, money and energy marketing to people you don't really want to serve.

This comes up a lot at networking events. People don't speak about their ideal client, they usually say something like 'I'm looking for anybody that wants xyz'. If you're looking for anybody, you will get anybody and those 'anybodies' may be real pains in the butt!

The more you can identify an ideal client, the more pleasurable your business becomes because you are working with ideal customers rather than just anybody.

Take the time to describe this person in full. Ask yourself things like:
- Who are they?
- What do they do for their income/business?
- Where do they work?
- Do they have kids?
- Are they male or female?
- What is their age?
- What are their hobbies?
- What do they watch on TV?
- What do they read?

Write down everything you can think of. You may have more than one ideal client so separate them out, because remember, when marketing to a female you will use different methods to a male. When marketing to a twenty-something you will use different methods, words, images to a fifty-something. Don't write down my ideal client is a female between twenty-five and fifty – that's too big a gap. Narrow it down to your ideal. Trust me, unless you state we are looking for twenty-five year old females only, you will still attract the other age groups. We just want to get in the head of your ideal client and understand them.

So the next step is to think about WHAT they want? If they were to buy from your business or to do business with you, what would they want?

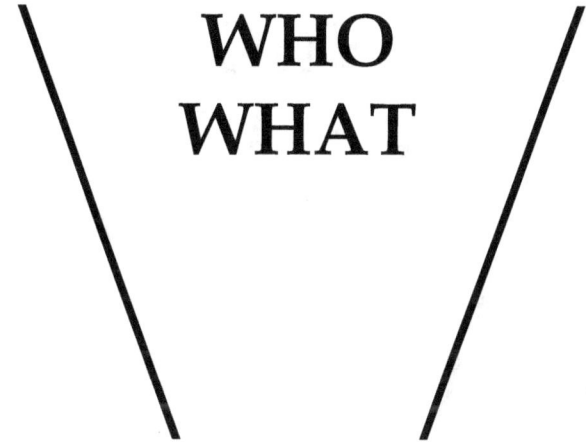

Let me give you an example. Let's say you are in a network marketing business and you have decided that your ideal distributor or partner would be a couple, newly married who want to have kids in the next year or two. What would they want from your business model?

They might want to know there is a guaranteed system. They might want to know you have integrity. Maybe they might want mentoring or education or access to resources. They might want to know you are friendly and they will have some fun whilst building their business in partnership with you.

The more you can list, the better. Because this leads to step three which is WHY you? Why would this ideal customer want to buy from you?

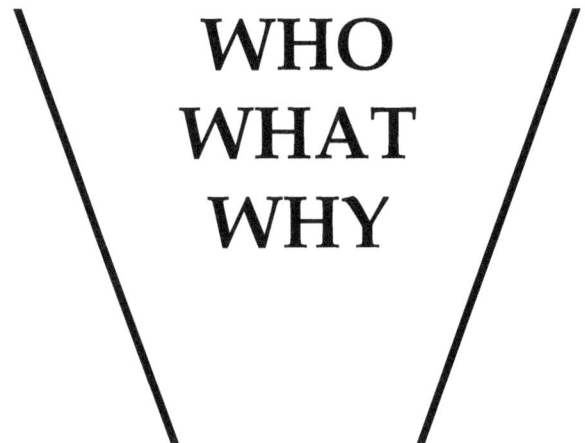

Firstly, you would want to make sure you cover all the 'whats'. Sometimes we can come up with an ideal customer, but in actual fact they want things you just can't offer. Maybe you said your ideal customer is a large company that manufactures items and as, for example, a VA (virtual assistant), you could help them, but then you realise they actually would like a full time personal assistant that works onsite. This means they don't actually want you and that's OK - you just have to go back to the start and work out a new ideal client that will.

Once you have ticked off the 'whats', I want you to think specifically why you or your business? Maybe you have some personal experience in the area. Maybe it's because of your previous results achieved or a specialized technique you use. Maybe it's as simple as your location. When I first started as a business coach, I marketed to the businesses in the street next to where I lived. I walked into businesses on a three block street. It wasn't even in the radius, it was just up and down three blocks of one street. Why me? Because I was local and I lived literally just around the corner.

This is usually where business owners will get stuck. They sometimes try to be too unique or they are far too general. If you are putting down something like "I have integrity" and "I'm honest", I don't think that they are highly unique because I would hope that all business owners have integrity and are honest. They could be items you write down, but may not be great marketing points. At the same time, you don't have to do something totally unique, you might just do something better than other people or something that no one else is talking about.

The other day on TV I saw an advertisement for a mattress company. They were talking about how they make their mattresses double sided so that you can 'flip' your mattress and get more use out of it and that it will last longer. I was amazed and in fact went to my bed to see if my mattress was double sided. It was, so I started to ask lots of people if their mattress was double sided. Amazingly, I haven't found anyone who's mattress is not double sided! This company took a common mattress feature that their ideal client wanted (a longer lasting mattress), and marketed it because no one else mentioned this fact. Sometimes the 'why you' is not all that unique, it's just that no one else has thought about what it is their ideal client would want.

Once you have worked out your "why you", we now think about the WHERE. Where would we find these ideal clients in their greatest concentration?

If we are going to take the time, money and energy to market, let's go to the place where all these ideal clients 'hang out' together. If you are looking for business owners, they are probably going to be at business networking groups or business seminars. If you are looking for Mums with kids, then you will probably find them at schools or kids sporting groups. If you are looking for ideal clients that like to keep fit, then you will find them at gyms or sporting clubs.

This is why you want to list out who your ideal client is in great detail. What are their hobbies? What do they do for work? By having a greater understanding about who your ideal client is, then you will make it easier to discover where you could find them.

Remember to also consider what other services or products this ideal client would purchase because this could also help you to discover where to find them. You are looking for businesses that have the same ideal client as you do, but they are not in competition with your business. For example, a hairdresser and a beauty therapist would most likely have the same ideal client, but they are not in competition with each other. If you were the hairdresser then the where for your ideal client could be at a local beauty therapist. A Virtual Assistant and an Accountant could have a similar ideal client, but they are not in competition with each other. If you were the Virtual Assistant, then the where for your ideal client could be at a local Accountant.

This final item on the list is usually what people start with when they think about marketing, but it is actually the last thing you work on. That is HOW do you best get in front of your ideal client.

A business owner may be offered a half price advertisement in a newspaper and they think, "I need more customers, this is a good deal, let's do it!", but they haven't stopped to think, would my ideal customer even read this paper?

When you are doing your marketing you want to get a return on investment. That is for the money, time and effort you spend on marketing you want it to produce more customers and profit than what it has cost you in marketing. If you go into marketing without a little thought, you might as well flush your money down the toilet. By understanding your ideal client you may even discover cheaper and easier marketing methods that produce a greater return on investment.

For example, you may have been placing an ad in the local paper and it has been costing you $1,000 a month to generate around the same amount of business. You then do the exercise to work out your ideal client and discover that they are likely to go to a weekly breakfast networking breakfast. The cost of the networking group is about $1,000 for the year and then through your test and measuring results it is bringing you referrals for your ideal client on a weekly basis at the value of more than the $1,000 each and every week!

One thing I would highly recommend for all home-based business owners is that you need to get out and network. Even if you are selling items online, you will find that a lot of your online sales will come from offline marketing. I am always amazed by who knows who. Your ideal client might not be at a networking event, but the person who knows or has a database full of your ideal clients could be there. The other reason is that networking events are cost effective, plus it puts you in an environment with other business owners which means you are getting out of the house and creating associations which are vital for your home-based business success.

So, marketing doesn't have to be as difficult as you think. Take the time to define who your ideal client is, what they would want, why they would want to buy it from you, where you find them in their greatest concentration and then finally how do you get in front of them.

Marketing is not about branding. Yes, you want to make sure you have a logo and you are consistent in your marketing, but you can't as a home-based business owner hope that people are going to come and buy from your business because you have put your logo somewhere. When you are marketing you are looking for direct response marketing. That is, your marketing should produce leads or enquiries to your business.

There is a lot more detail you can go into with marketing and how to 'fine tune' your ability to get in front of your ideal client, but this exercise of five simple questions is where I start with any marketing that I am planning.

A great idea would be to do this exercise for you own business. Not only does it help you in marketing your business, but it will also help you to become very clear about the type of people you want to work with and serve through your business.

PART 2: SKILL

Sales….

The second skill of business that I want to help you with is sales. Sales is one of those skills that you either love or hate. I haven't came across many people that fall somewhere in the middle of this. Even if you are great at sales and really love it, it is always worthwhile stopping and relearning the basics. When you do, you can sometimes find just one little tweak to your technique, and that one little tweak could result in just a percent or two increase in your conversion rate, that could then equate to a big increase in profit in your business.

So why is it that so many people dislike sales? When you think of a salesperson, who do you think of? I would guess that at least 80% of you reading this would have thought of a used car salesman or insurance salesperson or maybe even a door-to-door vacuum cleaner salesperson. When the majority of people think about having to sell, what they are actually thinking is that they will have to be some dodgy, pushy salesperson. This is as far from the truth as you can get.

Absolutely you can be a dodgy, product pushing salesperson, but I guarantee, that although you might make some sales in the short term, this is not good for your long term success in business.

What I'd suggest is that you <u>stop selling</u> and <u>start helping</u>. I don't know many people that like to be sold to, but I do know lots of people that like to buy. When you try and sell to people, they will try and resist. If you go in with the intention to truly help someone and then allow them to buy, you will find that sales become fun and easy.

In the end, sales is all about confidence. If you are going into a sales appointment, how confident you are will affect whether you make a sale or not. That being said, don't mistake confidence with arrogance. Confidence is going into a sale knowing that you want to help the potential buyer, that you believe in what it is you are offering them and that you can find a solution to their problems.

When I was in my early twenties and working as a Radiographer, I decided to give party plan a go. I did it more because I had no sales training and thought this would be a great training ground for me, plus I also loved the products of the company I was going to be a demonstrator for. I thought the worse that could happen is that I end up with a whole lot of their products.

I didn't realise at the time, but I came up with a winning strategy. I understood that at every party there would always be someone that was dragged to the party and even though they didn't want to buy anything, they also felt like they had too because they would be embarrassed at the end if they didn't place an order. Not because I was trying to sell more, but because it made me more confident for my demonstration, I would always start by telling people that if they were one of the people that was here to 'fill a seat' that weren't interested in buying anything, that the best item to buy was the $9.95 spatula. I would show it to them. I'd also tell them that even though it was the cheapest thing, it was actually a really good buy and I loved it – which I did.

This idea was an ice breaker to give me confidence, but because I was more confident and I immediately put everyone at ease and they didn't think I was there to push people into buying things they didn't want, the result was that I sold, much more than I would have otherwise.

PART 2: SKILL

You don't have to be a pushy person to sell. If you can find a need with your potential client, then and only then, do you have the opportunity to provide a solution to their need and allow them to buy.

If you are too slick in your sales, people can feel it a mile away. Think about it. Think about the last time someone tried to sell to you. Did you pick it before they even got to their close? Learn from their mistake. Think about the last time you had an awesome buying experience. What did the salesperson do to make it a great buying experience? How did they handle the sale?

The biggest thing to remember is to ask for the sale. You will need to ask someone if they are ready to buy from you. You can use lines such as 'So it sounds like xyz will solve this for you and correct me if I'm wrong, but it sounds like you are ready to go with xyz, is that right?' If they aren't ready to buy, they will let you know, but you are just stating a fact rather than pushing.

I have never loved sales or had much experience at it, but I have a high conversion rate in my sales appointments. Why? Because I only sell to people that want to buy. I always take the time to find a need and then allow them to buy by letting them know what I have for them to purchase and how that could help them. If I can't find a need, then I tell them straight out that I have nothing for them to buy, but if they know someone who needs what I do, then I'd love to help them. So even when I don't make a sale, I have a high conversion rate of gaining a referral – the best type of business lead.

Sales is one skill area that you need to become good at. It is the skill that will massively increase your success in your home-based business and most home-based business owners run micro businesses (they don't have any employees so that means they will be doing the majority of their own sales). If you double your conversion rate, (turning your leads or enquiries into sales) you will almost certainly double your profit.

If your sales are not at the level you would like them to be, maybe it is time to work on them. Start with your confidence and then ask yourself, how would your potential client like to buy. There are lots of tips and ideas on how to work on your sales process, but if you can start from the idea that you are aiming to help rather than sell, you are off to a great beginning. Add this to a passion and belief in what you 'sell' and you usually can't go wrong. The aim is not to sell ice to Eskimos, the aim is to find out if the Eskimos truly want to buy ice and allow them to buy it from you.

PART 2: SKILL

One last word on skills....

I have only looked at two basic skills in this book and only the starting points to help you with marketing and sales, but I truly hope that this has added value to you.

Remember my biggest tips on 'skills' is to firstly understand that you can learn a skill, any skill. The second is to start with the skills that you already display a talent in because these are easier to improve than your weaknesses. That being said, remember you still have to work on your weaknesses, especially if they will affect your business in a major way (such as marketing and sales). With a little common sense though, and by thinking about what is best for your potential customers, then you can absolutely succeed in your business.

Part 3:

MINDSET

Mindset

When the topic of mindset is mentioned, most people think that it's all about having a positive attitude. Although it is about having a positive attitude, I don't believe that's all it's about. There are more factors than just positive attitude that make up mindset.

When working in a home-based business, because the majority of the time you will be the only person running and working on your business, mindset is a key component and it is a component that only you can work on. It is definitely not something you can outsource!

What people believe to be true and what is the reality are often two very different things. Over my years working as a home-based business owner, and working with home-based business owners, I've discovered that many have a need for perfection. This is totally understandable and I've even done it myself. The reason is that there is no one else to hide behind. If you put out an email with errors or your delivery or distribution is delayed, or there is a mistake made on an account, there is no one to blame. You and everyone else know that it's your error.

For this reason, I find that home-based business owners in particular, have this need for perfection. The only problem with perfection is that it can lead to procrastination. That is, if it is not going to be perfect, a home-based business owner will in effect sit on the task or item until they can find a way to make it perfect. They will procrastinate or delay finishing a task, or even starting a task, because the end result will not be perfect.

This is an item that falls under mindset. We need to change or tweak our mindset because if you wait for everything to be perfect for your business to succeed, it will never even get off the ground. You don't have to have all the facts, all the knowledge, and all the skills before you get started. If this was the case, I'd still be an employee – what about you?

What I'd suggest is that you change you mindset just a little. Change the way you think. It is such a minor change, but it will help you get more things done and to build towards success. What I suggest is that you start to aim for excellence, rather than perfection.

In every area of your business, start to aim for excellence. This is basically lowering your bar for success. Excellence is not an outside measure, it is an internal measure. It is not for others to judge, it is for you to judge. Perfection is just too hard to achieve. I don't know about you, but while living life you have lots of balls in the air that you have to juggle. Business, family, friends, health or just life in general. I have never managed to be perfect in every area of my life at the same time – ever!

I am not suggesting that you do sub-standard work or that you do tasks in your business faster whilst compromising on quality. What I am suggesting is that you aim for excellence. That is, you do the best you can, but at the same time, don't stop and wait for it to be perfect before putting it out there.

I find this occurs mainly when home-based business owners are promoting or selling their goods or services. They think they need to have all the information, have all the facts, and be able to handle every single sales objection with the perfect line, before they get started. I believe you don't know what you are going to really need until you get started. It would be like trying to learn how to swim without getting in the water. Sometimes you need to just get out and get wet!

No one expects you to be perfect, so why do you expect it? We learn from our mistakes, right? So go make some mistakes faster so that you can learn faster. If you can turn your mindset around to believe that it is not only OK to make mistakes, but it is essential to your future success, then you can get on with it and go on to be successful.

The thought that helped me personally with this was to be really honest with myself. I stopped listening to all those doubting voices in my head and started to talk to myself in a logical manner. If I did make a mistake or maybe a huge error when servicing a client or in my business, am I the sort of person who would ignore the error? Would I blame someone else? Would I swear and yell about it? No to all of these things. If I made an error that involved a client, I know that it would be my personality to bend over backwards to fix the mistake and to apologise the whole time I was correcting the error – even if the client was the one yelling and swearing! Did I have enough belief in myself to realise that if I did make a mistake, that I could figure out a way to fix it? I have not yet come across a mistake that I have made that I have not been able to correct. Sometimes I didn't have the answers, but I also knew that I would know someone who could help me. Do you believe that to be true for yourself as well?

In the end, it comes down to the 80/20 rule. If you haven't heard of this rule before it is a rule that works in almost all areas of your life, not just business. You will find that 20% of your customers make 80% of your profit, 20% of your distributors will produce 80% of your sales, 20% of your database will produce 80% of your headaches. I like to use this rule to help me in my business. I figure that if I have 80% of the information or knowledge, I can figure out the other 20%. If I can get things right 80% of the time, then I am on track. If I need to make a decision and 80% of people would choose A and 20% would choose B, then I'll go with A. You are not aiming for 100%, you are aiming for 80%. Or in some cases you are not aiming for 100% , you are aiming for 20%. Imagine that you can work out and market to people who are like the 20% of your database that produce the most profit for your business, these are the ones you love to work with and sell to and help? How long would it be before 80% of your database were your ideal customers and only 20% were more of a 'basic' customer to you?

These examples I've used serve two points. The first is exactly as I have already explained. The second point is to realise that often times your mindset is actually just how you look at things or your perception of what is going on. For example, if it is a beautiful sunny day, one person might look at it and say, "Isn't it a beautiful sunny day?" Another person might just look at it and think, "I'm going to get sunburnt". It is the classic question – is the glass half full or half empty? This is where a positive attitude comes from.

PART 3: MINDSET

Do you know someone in your life that is negative all of the time? They are always complaining about something or they are telling you once again why it is someone else's fault that they are not succeeding. They can blame what is happening in their life on their neighbour, their work, the government, the weather – anything or anyone except themselves. My question to you is – do you like being around this person?

This hits close to home for me, because I believe that I was once one of these people. Nothing seemed to be going right for me. It seemed everyone was out to push me down and that all my issues in life were someone else's fault. It got to the point that one day I clearly remember standing at my workplace and saying, 'What do you have to do to get some attention around here, get a brain tumour?' That was a pretty stupid thing to say with the perspective of hindsight, and it takes a lot of courage for me to tell you this. Why? Because six months later I had a brain tumour. Now you understand why I believe in the law of attraction!

Why is it so crucial for me to tell you this story? Because once I was diagnosed with that tumour and faced with life or death, I had to make a decision. Was I going to step up and solve this problem or was I going to continue to complain and lay down and die – not just in theory, but actually die. Don't wait for a life or death situation to change your own mindset.

I started a journey of learning how to be more positive and how to become solution orientated. As an example, at one stage the medication I was on had the side effect of causing depression. My doctor hadn't informed me of this, so when I went to see him and told him that I was feeling a bit 'blue' he said it was the medication and started to write out a prescription for an anti-depressant. Well, by this stage I'd done enough work to realise that medicating a side effect of another medication would only lead to me taking extra pills to counter the side effects of the medication that countered the side effects of my actual medication! I said no and booked myself into a Psychologist to work out how I could overcome this depression without having to numb all my emotions – good and bad – with an anti-depressant.

My psychologist did think I was a little weird because my sessions would start with me explaining "This is what you taught me last time, and this is how I applied it". "These are the four books I've read in the last two weeks and this is what I learnt" and then "These are my questions for today". Let's just say I was a little different to the average client that was looking to blame someone else for all their problems in their life. In the end, I knew that the problems in my life were mine, and mine alone.

I haven't told you this story to make it sound like I am some sort of positive attitude guru. I've told you this story so that you realise that having a positive attitude is not a natural state for me. In fact, I am naturally very pessimistic. I have learnt to have a positive attitude. I did the work to ensure that I now 'default' to a positive attitude. The best thing is, my life is so much better when I look at it with a positive attitude. You too can change your attitude, if you are willing to do the work.

PART 3: MINDSET

Don't fool yourself into thinking that a positive attitude means that your life or business will be perfect. In fact, I have just as many problems as you probably do. The difference between someone with a positive attitude compared to someone with a negative attitude, is that the positive attitude person looks for a solution, they take control and steer the ship. If you are working in a home-based business, whatever that business is, if you don't start working with a positive, 'can do' attitude, you may as well 'close up shop'.

I learnt this the hard way and in an extreme circumstance by being diagnosed with a brain tumour, but today, I am so thankful that I did get the tumour. Without getting that tumour, my life would not be where it is today. That tumour was a blessing in disguise because it changed the course of my life.

Sometimes when things go wrong in life, we are too quick to judge it. At the time of the tumour it was horrible, but now with time I can be grateful for it. This is what I mean by having perspective. When in the situation, don't judge it. It is what it is. Life is going to throw curve balls at you every day of the week – big and small. These curve balls are just an opportunity for you to stand back and look for a better answer and a better solution.

In your home-based business, you need to come from the place of a positive attitude or a 'can do' attitude, a mindset that you can work it out. I think this is even more important for home-based business owners than for people working in a large workforce, because in the end, there is no one else to save you. It's up to you!

You need to learn personal responsibility. This is something that I speak about when I am doing keynote presentations because, from my experience, the only person you are 100% responsible for is yourself. So many people like to believe that they can push off their responsibility to others (which is usually in the form of blaming others) but in the end, the buck stops with you. If you want to take your home-based business to the next level of success that you desire and you want to achieve that burning desire, your 'why', then take on more personal responsibility. You can handle it!

It is how we react and respond to situations that make the difference in our lives. You can react to a failure by sitting in the corner crying about it, or you can learn from your mistakes and what went wrong and then go try again. You can react to a difficult situation with fear, anger or even not face it at all, or you can react to the situation with poise, grace and a problem solving attitude. Remember the saying, 'It's not what happens to you, but how your react to it that matters'. This is your mindset. It is all about you making the choice on how you will react and respond to situations and events – and not just negative situations and events. How you react and respond when things are going well is just as important as how you react and respond when they aren't.

Failure is again just a matter of perspective with your mindset. One of the biggest fears of most business owners is that they will fail. For some it is small failure that paralyses them, for others it is grand monumental failure. What I'm about to share with you is probably not the text book answer, but this is what I have found that works.

PART 3: MINDSET

The first thing is to simply accept that if you are in business you will fail at something, at sometime. Probably every day of the week something is not going to work as planned, or maybe not work at all. When people think of failure, they start to put that term on things that are really only things not working out or mistakes made. Failure is not as bad as you think.

The first thing I do is redefine what failure is to me. Failure to me is doing something that is out of my integrity or doing harm to another person intentionally. Failure to me is having my family disown me. Failure is giving up when all signs point to the fact that with some work I could turn an error or a situation around.

The other thing I do is I look at the worst case scenario. The facts are that more than 80% of businesses will fail in the first two years of operation. When you look further at these businesses, you will find that they don't fail because they are losing money, often times they fail because the business owner simply gave up. The business owner was too proud to ask for help, or to change their ways and look for a new way to do things, or that the business owner simply ran out of steam.

For me to succeed in business, I have to let go of thoughts of failure and replace it with the fact that some things work and others things don't. I like to think of the worst case scenario. OK, so what if my business does 'fail' and I do lose all my money. Well, I know my Mum would give me a place to live. I know that I could go and get a job. I worked at McDonald's as a part-time manager when I was at University, I'm sure I could do so again. If the truth is to be told, I could probably go and get a high paying executive job somewhere. People offer me jobs all the time, but that's not what I want for myself. However, if I had no other option I would work it out. I would survive.

I think when people have this thought of failure, they think that it is like a big black hole that they will never return from. The biggest issue with perceived failure is not the actual events that went wrong, but our self image and our belief in who we are. You need to become like a duck. Failure needs to become like water off a ducks back – it just slides off. Success is just getting up one more time than falling down.

Persistence is going to become your best friend in your business. To succeed in business you need to keep going. Don't blindly keep doing the same things over and over. You must gain education and ask for help with things that are not going according to plan, or working out the way you want them too. But firstly you have to decide to keep going at all.

If you are not educating yourself in your business and life, then you will have trouble building your home-based business. You can give me examples of business owners that don't read, don't attend seminars, watch TV and listen to the radio in the car rather than listening to an educational audio, but I would really like to know if their journey to success would have been easier and faster if they had educated themselves along the way. I believe it would have!

One of my favourite sayings is 'Life is too short to learn from just your own mistakes, learn from everyone else's as well'. This is why I've shared some of my stories with you. I want you to really learn from my errors so that you don't have to go through what I went through to get to where I am. The best way to learn from others is to educate yourself. Read books, listen to audios, attend seminars. With the internet, it now makes it even easier to learn with online programs with 24 hour, worldwide access. You don't need to have a mentor that you physically sit with and talk to, although that would be ideal. You can have a mentor from reading their book or watching a video of them speaking.

I find that if I am reading a minimum of 15 minutes each and every day it helps me keep a positive mindset. Remember, I am not naturally positive so therefore I must work on it daily to keep it in check. Just as I have to with my health. I have to walk daily to make sure I don't add massive weight – another delightful side effect of my medication. Is it hard to read for 15 minutes or is it hard to walk for 30 minutes – especially when I walk on the beach? No, it's not hard. The question is not if it is hard or if it is worthwhile, it's "Are you going to do it?"

I could talk on this topic of mindset in home-based business for days, but here is the one point that I think the majority of home-based business owners, or any business owners, struggle the most with. It is not about having a positive attitude or taking personal responsibility or even taking the time to further their education. I find that the greatest struggle of mindset comes from giving yourself permission to succeed. It's your belief in yourself.

In society, we hear all those warnings about not being selfish, about not getting 'too big for your boots', about not thinking too much of yourself, or worse still telling everyone how good you are. Because we have these pressures from society to conform and not to become the tall poppy, we will often play down our success. We will be subconsciously sabotaging our success because we don't want to be 'that person' in the world that people talk about behind their back or, as is the case now, on Facebook or on their website or blog.

There is only one person who can get you the success that you desire. You. This is the exact same person who is the only person who can give you the permission to go and make it happen. I know I have personally cared for so long what other people think, and it was just this year that I decided that this was a really energy zapping way to live my life. In the end, if they thought that I was crazy or that I talked too fast or that I was overweight or that they didn't like me, why spend all my energy on trying to please these people or trying to stay off their 'radar'. They weren't sitting here in my home whilst I worked at making my life better. They weren't going to help me create an environment where I could help parents make an income for their family and care for their kids at the same time with a home-based business. In fact, these people that I was so consumed with, were actually stopping me from doing what I needed to do. Not actually them, but the thought of them.

I read in a book once that people think 10,000 times more about themselves than they do anyone else. Wow! That is a lot. So if someone does have one thought about me, it's only 0.01% of their thoughts for the day!

In the end, look inside of yourself. Are you a good person? Do you want to care for your family? Do you want to run a good, honest business with integrity? Do you want to do good to, or for others? Do you believe that you don't want to intentionally harm others? If this is true for you, then stop listening or even thinking about the people in the world that want to pull you down. Ultimately, this is there problem and not yours. As long as you are always looking to add value to others – whether it's your clients, business partners, friends or family – then I honestly believe you can't go wrong.

PART 3: MINDSET

I'd suggest that at least 10% of people that read this book will probably not like it. In fact, they may even hate it and believe it was a waste of their time. If that is true then at least 10% of people that read this book will love it and it will make a huge difference in their life and business. They will be grateful that I put myself 'out there' and wrote it. So who should I focus on? The bottom 10% who hate it or the top 10% who love it? It sounds very logical when you read it here right?

My question to you is this. Are you focusing on the bottom 10% who dislike you, no matter how good you are, or what you do, or are you focusing on the top 10% who need you to do what you do to help them? Stop being selfish and holding back your success because I guarantee you, you will have 10% of people, at least, that don't like you or disagree with you. Don't allow them to stand in the way of your success. Focus instead on the 10% (at least), who really need you to step up and build your business because they need and want you. I don't care what your business is, you will be helping someone, even in a small way. It is time that you give yourself permission to achieve your 'why'.

This is why is it so important to connect with, read, look at and remind yourself of your 'why' each and every day and if possible more than once a day. Stay focused on who will benefit from your success not on the people who want to pull you down. If you are a parent, this is one of the best things you can teach your children. Remember they learn from what you do, not what you say, so go be a success and teach them that you can be a successful person in business and be a great parent and do the right thing by people. Imagine who they will grow up to be if you are leading your family with this as an example?

Part 4:

ACTION

ACTION

Something that is not always discussed, but is vital to any business, is the actions you take. It is great to have a rock solid mindset with a high belief that not only can you succeed, but that it is OK to succeed. It is great to have all the skills in the world and that you know your stuff back to front. It is awesome to have a burning desire and a 'why' that you are working to achieve, but if you decide to sit on your couch and watch TV, you are never going to achieve your 'why'. You won't be using those amazing skills and your mindset will be left to deteriorate whilst you fill your mind with the 'garbage' on TV. If you are not willing to do the work to gain success in your home-based business, don't start.

As harsh as this sounds, by this stage of reading this book, if you are not fired up to go out there and give your business a red hot go, then you probably never will be. You may have it all perfected in your head, but you need to get out there. You need to 'get in the water' so that you can start to experience your business and learn how to swim. Standing on the banks and watching everyone else swim is no fun!

There is more to action than just jumping in the deep end and throwing your arms around trying to stay afloat. A great analogy for this is a rocking horse. On a rocking horse there is a lot of action, but you are not going anywhere. Action for the sake of action, or work for the sake of work, is not necessarily the answer.

Because a lot of home-based business owners choose to operate their business in and around a job, there is one key thing you need to do. You need to treat your home-based business as a <u>real</u> business. I don't care if your business is something you do one night a week or one that is full time. You must treat it like a real business rather than just something you do. A business is run to make profit. You need to allocate time to not only do the work that is the business, but you need to also allocate time to do the work on your business that will make it grow.

Let me give you an example. Two types of businesses that are ideal part time businesses for a home-base are party plan businesses and network marketing businesses, yet both of these businesses are the most likely to fall into the category where people are doing 'this thing', or they are doing just a few parties. It is something they sort of just 'add in'. They are not treating it like a real business – but they are real businesses. The work <u>in</u> the business may be doing a party demonstration or sharing an opportunity with a prospect, but the work <u>on</u> the business is setting goals, strategic planning the future and to increase your profit margins. Your home-based business should not be something you do, it should be something that you own and run. There is really a subtle difference in this wording, but it makes a huge difference to where you business will end up.

PART 4: ACTION

To treat your home-based business like a business, you need to act like the owner of your business, which firstly means talking about your business like an actual business. Think about the last time you were at a gathering on the weekend. Did you talk proudly about your business or did you sort of mention you were doing this 'thing' part-time. I know I've done that. You want to get to a place where you talk about your business like someone that is running a multi-million dollar corporation. It doesn't have to be boastful, but you should be proud.

The second thing you need to do is treat your home-based business like a real business by allocating your time. Even if your business is not a full time endeavor, that doesn't mean it should be relegated to your spare time. If it can only be done during your spare time then I wish you luck, because in today's world, I don't know many people with spare time. Make it a part-time business which therefore means you need to set aside your time to work your business.

Some home-based business owners make their own merchandise and sell it at a market on a Sunday. If you are out selling your items, then treat it like a business, not a spare time hobby. To do this, you need to have a plan.

Now I am not a fan of business plans. Why? Because when most people do a business plan they have this in depth business plan that is pages and pages of information that gets all typed up beautifully and then bound in a folder, which then gets put on a shelf to spend its life collecting dust!

When you are in a home-based business you will find that you need to be more fluid in your plans. Tomorrow you could be presented with an amazing business opportunity that could make your beautiful, thirty page business plan obsolete. This does not mean you shouldn't have a plan. It is more about the type of plan you should create. You need to develop a plan that can adapt to the changes in your business as they occur.

To get the best action in your home-based business you should have a basic plan to know what you should be working on, which direction you are headed and what you will need. Let's use the example that I am going to drive from my home on the Gold Coast to Sydney, which is about a ten hour drive south. Now I don't need to know every inch of the road on that journey, but it would be good to have a plan.

First of all, which direction am I heading. For a start, I go the half a block to the main road. Now if I turn right, I will not get to Sydney, I'd be going the wrong direction. From the very first minute of my journey, I could be going the wrong way. I see this all the time in business. From the start of their business, they are going the wrong way. They haven't worked out their 'why' and the first step to achieve it.

On my drive to Sydney, do you think it would be a good idea to have in my plan where I will need to stop and refuel my car? Where should I plan to stop and get fuel because I don't want to run out of fuel halfway between towns in the middle of nowhere, right? So in your business, where will you need to stop driving for a few minutes and refill your fuel. This might mean stopping and realising you have gone as far as you can on what you knew, and that now it is time to stop and ask for help or gain some new information.

PART 4: ACTION

Would it be good to check out the weather conditions before heading off on a long road trip? Is there any road closures on my journey? Often times home-based business owners start on their journey in business, but don't look to see where the road blocks are or could potentially be. If you know there is a potential block in your business road, wouldn't it be good to anticipate that and find an alternate route before hitting the block? It would be a good idea to find out if there are any stormy conditions in your industry, new laws, new economic times or new technology due to come onto the market.

I could use this one analogy for a whole day and I'm sure you can think of some too, but I just want you to realise that before you start working on your business and heading for your 'why', you need to have some sort of plan. How many customers do you need? How much will they pay you on average? How many enquiries do you think you will need to get that number of customers to buy? What are your expenses? When you get to a particular profit level in your business, what will you need to do to go to the next level?

These are not hard things, but you would be surprised at how many people don't have any idea or even a basic plan for their business. It is vital for your success otherwise you can be doing a lot of work and taking lots of actions, but still be heading in the wrong direction or the work you are doing is not helping you grow your business. This is when people are busy being busy, but not achieving!

Time management

Time management is vital for the home-based business owner. To be more precise we should be calling it 'personal management' because personally I can't manage time! The clock continues to tick whether or not I want it to. There is always 24 hours in a day. I haven't found some magic time machine that can add or subtract hours in a day. It is not time we need to manage, it is how we use the time available that we need to manage.

I think of time management strategies a bit like a smorgasbord. There are so many different techniques, ideas and theories on how to manage your time best, but because it is about personal management rather than time management, I think it is finding the strategy that works best for you.

A couple of my favourites range from very simple ideas through to full on management. Let's start with an easy one and work our way up. These are just a couple of ideas for you to trial and see what works best for you.

Generally what happens with a home-based business owner is that they lose track of time. Have you had a day like that? It is four in the afternoon and you started working at eight in the morning and you all of a sudden think, "What did I actually do today? Where has the time gone?" The challenge is that we can get caught up in what we are doing, but after a period of time we are no longer working effectively. I would suggest something as simple as setting an alarm clock.

PART 4: ACTION 79

You can use the timer on your oven, an alarm on your mobile phone or anything that you can set to make an audible sound after a period of time. Set you timer to go off in one hour. When the timer goes off, take a moment and ask yourself, is this activity I'm doing the best use of my time? It really is that simple, because when the alarm goes off, it wakes you up. It lets you know that an hour has passed – which can feel like five minutes – so that you can get back on track to what needs to be done. Then simply reset your alarm to go off in another hour and continue for the whole day.

Another thing you can do is set yourself what I refer to as a 'not-negotiable hour'. This would ideally be each day, but if you are struggling with daily, aim for a minimum of at least once a week. I want you to imagine that I have a one hour appointment booked with you. I am flying to your location and you are paying me a lot of money for this appointment. Would you miss this appointment with me? Unless there was a real emergency, I doubt you would just not show up. The problem is, how often are you not showing up for an appointment you set with yourself? I guarantee you, an appointment with yourself is more important for your business than meeting with anyone else, because without you there is no business. That's why this time slot should be not-negotiable. You don't swap it for anything unless it is an absolute emergency.

Now the practicalities of this is to make sure you schedule this hour at a time when you are least likely to be interrupted. Don't make it for the time when you are most likely to get a lot of phone calls, or at a time that is your 'prime time' to be out selling. Do realise though that one hour is enough time, if uninterrupted, to get a lot done. Turn off your phone during this time. If you had to go to the doctor for an hour your phone would be off. People can leave a message. Remove all distractions or possible distractions so that you can maximize this not-negotiable hour.

I find this not-negotiable hour not only helps you get more done, it starts to put you into control of your business. Don't forget too that you can use this same idea outside of your business as well. Maybe you can have a not-negotiable hour to spend with your kids, or a not-negotiable hour for exercise or a not-negotiable hour to do something else you love to do.

At the other end of the scale is the full on version of personal management – the deliberate diary. That is, you have a weekly schedule of when you work on things and allocate this time in the week. Think when you were at high school, you didn't have to worry about time management, your day was scheduled. You knew that at ten on a Tuesday you had English in room three and then at eleven you would have Science in room six and so on. You didn't have to think each week where you would fit in your three hours of English or your four hours of science. You can do the same for your business. You may allocate from ten to eleven on a Monday to work on your marketing. From one to three you may do a sales appointment. On a Tuesday, from nine to ten, you may do all your invoicing.

PART 4: ACTION

The theory behind this works. A deliberate diary does work. The challenge is if you don't follow it. The other challenge is if you schedule every minute you have available to work. I don't know about you, but I can pretty much guarantee everyday that something will come up that needs to be attended to that was not on my to do list when I started my day. If you don't allow time for this, you will find your deliberate diary will not work.

It can be too overwhelming and too scheduled for some people so you might need to work up to it. I started with what I called theme days. Monday was my administration day, Tuesday was my appointment day, Wednesday was my coaching day and Friday was my education and planning days.

You will note that I didn't put in Thursday. I don't like working Thursday. I have no idea why, but it just seems on a Thursday I don't seem to work very well, so I don't. I have Thursday off. It is after all my business and I can choose what I do. I usually go to a breakfast meeting on a Thursday and allow time to chat with someone from the group for an hour after, and then my day is done. I have my phone on and check my emails, but I don't work unless I feel like it. It is amazing though how much work you can get done on the other days when you put in your days off.

If I wanted to, I could work seven days a week from six in the morning to ten at night, but is it productive? I actually love working on a Sunday morning. To the employee minded people that is 'wrong'. You don't work Sunday, it's the weekend, it's a day off. I on the other hand don't label days with what is right or wrong. On a Sunday morning because no one calls or emails me and it kind of feels like a 'bonus' work day, I can get more done in four hours than I can in two or three days during the week. In fact, I often find that I get nearly all my work done on a Sunday morning and then the rest of the week I spend on chatting to people, emails or phone calls, and living my life. My Sunday morning is absolutely more productive than a Thursday for me.

Some of you might find that you work best from eight to eleven at night. If that is more productive for you, work at that time and sleep in. That is the beauty of a home-based business, it doesn't have to be nine to five. If you want to spend Tuesday afternoon taking your kids to sport, then do it. That being said, do set yourself 'work hours' or otherwise you will find you are working all of the time. Also remember, when you are 'at work', then work. When you are off or 'at home', then be off or at home.

This comes down to discipline. Lots of potential home-based business owners tell me they couldn't work from home because they are not very disciplined. They won't be able to work because they will be distracted at home by the things they need to do when at home like the housework. In reality, I find it is actually the reverse. It is the discipline not to work that you need!

PART 4: ACTION

Interesting right? It is far too easy to pop into your office to just check an email or send an invoice and then find yourself four hours later still working at your desk. Unlike people who have to travel to their workplace away from home, you never really ever leave the office. You need to start forming a discipline to have work times and home times. Once you gain this discipline, including talking about your business over the dinner table during family time, then home-based business is much, much easier.

When I first started working from home I lived in an apartment with a designated study. The beauty of this was that I could close the door and just be at home. The simple idea of having a door and a separate room meant that I could create a barrier between work and home. Working from your kitchen table is not ideal for your family life. At the very least, aim to have a desk or better still, one of those desks that close up like a cupboard or a roll top desk. These work fantastically because you can close them as you would a separate room. At the very least, try to have a box with all your work in it that you clean off the kitchen table and put away.

As you progress in your home-based business and form the discipline to stop, you will find it is easier to work wherever you want.

When I moved to the Gold Coast into a new apartment, I was going to set my office up in the spare bedroom. That was my original thought. When I started to move in, I realised that the spare bedroom was a bit hot and the window looked into the apartment building next door. On the other hand the front corner of the apartment, which is actually my lounge room, had two views out over the street and the garden. If I opened the window I could actually hear the waves at the beach just a two minute walk away. The light was good and there was air conditioning. I don't suggest this for everyone, but I set up my desk in the corner of my lounge room. If anyone was coming to my home, they knew I work from home so I didn't care what it looked like. I was now disciplined enough in my time management that I can easily sit on the couch and watch a movie without feeling the guilt that I 'should' be working. If you are new to home-based business, I don't recommend this, but for me, it put me in an environment that was enjoyable to work from and as a result, I am more productive.

Look at the space you have allocated for 'work'. Does it inspire you to work? Even if you are running a business that doesn't require a work space, you should at the very least have a desk. You will need to check emails and write your plans and keep your educational material, so get yourself a desk and set up your work space. I love to do my planning outside, so you will often find me sitting on my deck with a cuppa, often times still in my PJ's, working away. This is why I work from home. Working in a suit in a cubicle is not for me. I love to see the sky and feel the breeze. I am not distracted, I'm empowered to work.

To get the best action from yourself in your home-based business, look at where and how you work. With a few little tweaks and managing how you use the time available, you will gain better results in your home-based business.

Work Ethic

The reason a lot of home-based business owners don't succeed is because they lack work ethic. What is work ethic? I like to think of it as knowing that you have to do the work to get the success, and understanding that when you are working you actually need to work, not fluff around, pretending or deluding yourself that you are working.

I find that most employees will generally only work at about 80% of their actual capacity. Again it's the 80/20 rule. They often do this because if they work at 100% and something arises and they need to do extra, then they will be expected to work at 110% capacity. People without a strong sense of work ethic will usually do the minimal amount required to 'appear' that they are doing 100%, when in actual fact they are working at 80%. As a home-based business owner you can't afford to do this. There is no one to pay your wage. It is up to you.

Before you jump to conclusions, this does not mean that you are working 100 hours a week. It is about being effective in your work, rather than just doing lots of it. It is about making sure you are doing the things that will make a difference or to get results in your business.

I'm afraid, because I have worked for myself for so long, I get totally frustrated in the corporate world. It appears to me that many people have meetings just for the sake of having meetings. If a decision needs to be made, they will have six weeks of internal studies and ten meetings to make a decision I could make in about two seconds. Home-based business is not a democracy, it is a dictatorship. You make the decisions. You can waste a lot of time having meetings. If you do need to have a meeting with others, then have an agenda. Schedule it with a start *and* finish time.

Work ethic is all about not being afraid to do the 'dirty jobs' in your business. It is also about knowing what to do, and what is a waste of time. It is knowing that sometimes you will need to just do the work to get the result. Maybe, for example, the best way to gain new customers is to do some telemarketing for your business. I don't know about you, but I absolutely loathe even the thought of telemarketing, but it needed to be done so I did it. Now, I have work ethic and I will work hard and do what it takes, but if I have to do something I don't like, I'm going to make it count. When I first started as a coach, I conducted a telemarketing campaign. My goal was to find two new clients. So I made nine phone calls, secured five appointments and then signed on three new clients. If I was going to do the work then I was going to make it count! I'm a little smarter now and have a better cash position so I outsource all of my telemarketing to my VA who loves doing it. (Yes, I think she is 'weird' too!) Work ethic is not necessarily about doing lots of work, it is about working efficiently and effectively.

That being said, in some businesses you just have to do the numbers. If you are a VA (Virtual Assistant), you might find you need to meet with five business owners to gain one new regular customer. So the work ethic here is if you know you need five regular customers, how fast can you go sit in front of twenty-five business owners? Will you have the work ethic and the drive to do the numbers? Every business has their numbers so the faster you can work out yours and do the work required, the faster you will have the success in your business.

PART 4: ACTION

In the end, when running a home-based business you need to be what I term a 'self starter'. You can't wait for someone to hand you the work or expect that the phone will just ring. You need to get out and make your business work. You can't procrastinate all day long pretending to do work that in reality is never going to produce results for your business. You need to focus and make it happen!

The reason many people procrastinate is because they are in fear. They are avoiding doing what they know is right for them, and their business. This is why you need to make sure you have a clear 'why' for your business. If your 'why' is strong and can bring tears to your eyes and it is like a churn or a burn in your soul, then you will find you won't procrastinate. You will find you will be out making your business happen.

If you do find you are a bit of a procrastinator, then what do you do when you procrastinate? I found at one stage in my business that if I was procrastinating, I would lean back in my chair and look at the corner in the ceiling. So I got up on a stool and posted a note in the corner of the ceiling that simply said 'Are you procrastinating?' Wow, that stopped me in my tracks. If you find you head to the fridge to just grab a quick drink, which leads to doing the dishes, and then the washing, and then maybe a spot of channel surfing on the TV, then put a note on your fridge, or in a worst case scenario, padlock it!

Don't wait for someone, or something external to motivate you to do what is required to grow your home-based business into a success, you have to make it happen. You have to be inspired by your own dreams, goals, aspirations and your 'why' to make it happen. This is why I call it being a 'self starter'. You have to turn the key in your engine to get it running, don't wait for someone to come with jumper leads to jump start your engine every day.

My final point in action is to remember that consistency is the key. Short bursts of start/stop work will not produce significant results in your business. Consistent work ethic over time will produce massive results in your business, and your life. You can't run ten kilometers a day for a week, once a year and expect that you are going to be fit for the whole year. It is more like that a short twenty minute walk every day will produce the result of being fit for the entire year. The same thing will be true in your business. One week of flat out work will not produce the same results as consistently working even just an hour a day, every day on your business. Consistency will produce a greater result every time.

To super charge your results, if you do put in a short term 'burn' on your business and pair this with consistent work from that 'burn', you will see massive results. It is a bit like an airplane taking off. It will use massive energy and the engines at full throttle to take off, but that doesn't mean once in the air they turn the engines off. The engines remain on to continue the flight, but they are no longer at full throttle. Know when you need to work hard in your business and know when it is OK to just have consistent work ethic.

FINAL WORDS

In Conclusion

As we draw to the end of the journey we have shared in the pages of this book, I really hope that it has added value to you and your home-based business. I hope that it has given you the permission to succeed and to focus on what is really important to you.

I love working from home. Each day that I work in or on my business I can't help but smile and know that this is what I love to do. When I simplified what really needed to happen, it made my business so much more enjoyable.

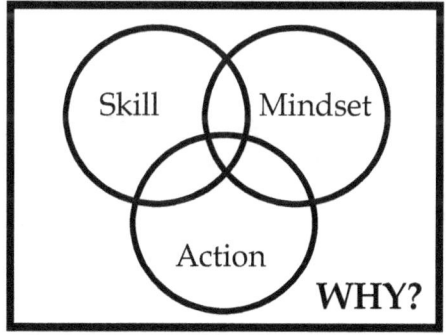

Remember that when you focus on developing your skills in business, choosing a positive mindset and taking the actions required to build your business you will gain success. The most important thing to keep these three areas working together is to border them – frame them with your 'why'. It is your 'why' that will be the difference between whether you succeed or not. A 'why' will fuel you to take the action needed for your home-based business. A 'why' will help you look at situations differently so that you react and respond in a way that will help you rather than hinder your success. A 'why' will help you uncover your natural talents and the areas where you need to develop your skills.

I believe in this simple formula that I created for my own success, in business and in life.

Right Attitude

+

Work Ethic

+

Focus

=

Success

FINAL WORDS

For me (and hopefully for you too), I believe that if I have the right attitude, it will help me gain the success I desire. When I say the right attitude, I don't mean that there is one right attitude for each individual and one wrong one. It simply means that there is a right attitude and that it can vary from person to person. It's this right attitude that is going to help you move forward.

Add the right attitude to your work ethic and success is far more achievable. Having a great attitude but not doing the work required will never lead to success. Affirmations not followed up with work are simply hopes. Affirmations with work applied can create miracles.

Then we need to remain focused. We live in a world of bright shiny objects and new opportunities being presented to us every second day – sometimes even more often than that – and it is so easy to be distracted from what we really want.

Remember that your 'why' is your personal 'why'. It is what you want. Don't allow someone else to come in and tell you what you should want. It is not about them, it is about you. You don't have to drive a flash car or have a big house to be successful. You don't need to have your photo on the cover of a magazine. Your success can only be defined by you.

When you combine these three simple things together, you are on the path to achieving your success, whatever that may be for you. This is not the time to give up on your dreams and goals. To be a success in your home-based business you need to keep going. When I feel down or things aren't going my way, (because sometimes they don't), I just repeat to myself over and over – just keep going, just keep going.

Your business is the vehicle to provide you with the lifestyle you want. Don't be the person that doesn't allow that vehicle to ever leave the garage. Home-based business, like any business, requires a leap of faith. You need to stick your neck out and give it a go. Trust me, it can be the best thing you ever do and it is a wonderful way to work and live. I now get to choose when I work, and how I work, and most of the time it is in my PJ's or some other very casual outfit. I am not sitting in a car in peak hour traffic wondering where my life is going. It will allow me when I have kids to be a full time mother, but at the same time still feel like it is not my only purpose in life, and that I can have a business and be a mum at the same time. It means that with a laptop, internet connection and a phone, my business can run from anywhere in the world. This is how I love to live.

Your picture of life may be different to mine, and that's OK. What is important is that you have a picture of how you want to live your life, and how your home-based business can help you achieve that. Once you have a plan in place, work the plan and make it happen.

Why not, just for the next year, give yourself permission to make it work? Why not do what it takes to build your business? Why not put in a little extra time to learn some new skills or develop your existing talents? Why not take a little extra time to educate yourself further in business? Why not? It could produce massive results. If you can't find a reason *not* to do this, then congratulations, your success is within reach.

FINAL WORDS

Thank you for helping me achieve my dreams and my 'why'. By simply reading this book you have helped my 'why'. Don't you think there are people out there who want to help you as well?

So until we meet someday – and I do hope that I get to meet you in person one day – keep looking for ways that you can add value.

Tracy

Want more?

Check out Tracey's online program just for home-based business owners....

www.theartofhomebasedbusiness.com/online

Would you like to get started in your own home-based business?

Would you like to take your home business to the next level?

Come visit us today at:
www.TheArtOfHomeBasedBusiness.com

- **FREE e-book** on 'Which Home-Based Business?' The guide to help you choose the home-based business that is best for you.
- **FREE e-magazine** each month packed with great information to help you in your home-based business
- **The Art of Home Based Business Online Course** developed to further assist home-based business owners – particularly with getting more customers – to build and grow their business (www.theartofhomebasedbusiness.com/online)
- Tracey regularly **blogs** on topics to add value to the home-based business owner
- **FREE videos** with hints and tips to help you further in your business.

www.TheArtOfHomeBasedBusiness.com

www.ingramcontent.com/pod-product-compliance
Lightning Source LLC
Chambersburg PA
CBHW061514180526
45171CB00001B/169